Enjoy!
Susan Schrempf

simple
Silk Ribbon
Embroidery
BY Machine

Step-by-Step Techniques for
Beautiful Embellishments

Susan Schrempf

C&T PUBLISHING

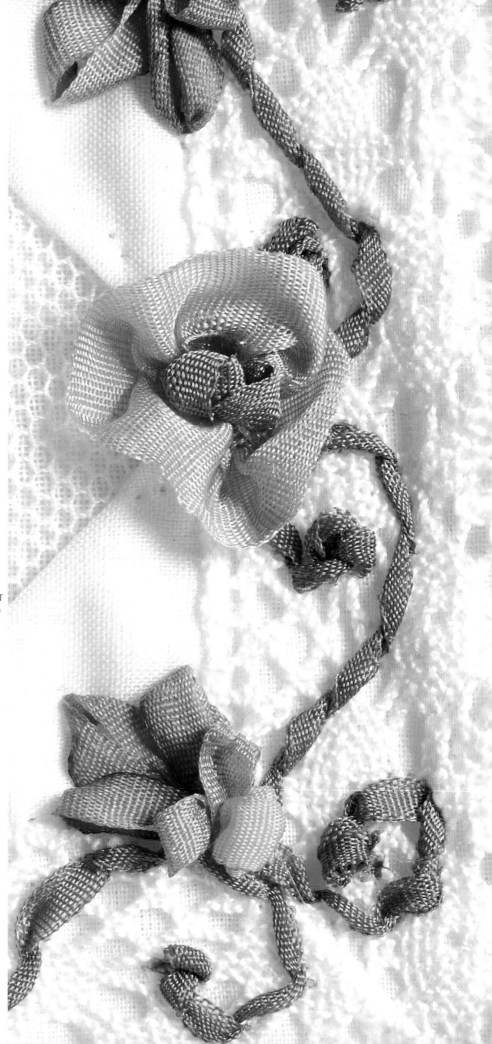

Text copyright © 2008 by Susan Schrempf

Artwork copyright © 2008 by C&T Publishing, Inc.

Publisher: Amy Marson

Editorial Director: Gailen Runge

Acquisitions Editor: Jan Grigsby

Editors: Susan Beck and Kesel Wilson

Technical Editors: Nanette S. Zeller and Susan Nelsen

Copyeditor/Proofreader: Wordfirm Inc.

Design Director/Cover & Book Designer: Christina D. Jarumay

Production Coordinator: Tim Manibusan

Illustrator: Tim Manibusan and Joshua A. Mulks

Photography by C&T Publishing, Inc., unless otherwise noted

Published by C&T Publishing, Inc., P.O. Box 1456, Lafayette, CA 94549

Library of Congress Cataloging-in-Publication Data

Schrempf, Susan,

  Simple silk ribbon embroidery by machine : step-by-step techniques for beautiful embellishments / Susan Schrempf.

    p. cm.

  ISBN-13: 978-1-57120-449-3 (paper trade : alk. paper)

  ISBN-10: 1-57120-449-0 (paper trade : alk. paper)

 1. Silk ribbon embroidery. 2. Machine embroidery. I. Title.

TT778.S64S35 2008

746.44'7041--dc22

                                        2007020443

Printed in China

10 9 8 7 6 5 4 3 2

contents

acknowledgments

Thank you,

My dear husband and true partner, who constantly exhibits the patience of more than one or two major saints. It is a special person who knows when to back off or jump in as needed for my mood swings.

My beautiful daughter, Sandra Clark—it is a lucky woman who has a friend and peer for a daughter. You are a fiber artist and writer in your own right, and I rely on you heavily. Your gentle nudging has made this book a reality.

My dearest friend, Jean Marble, who rides with me on my roller-coaster lifestyle—you are my confidant and proofreader.

Sulky of America educators Pat Welch and Suzy Seed, whose appreciation and support of my work has fed my spirit to persist. Your guidance has been invaluable.

Martha Pullen — your TV shows initiated my love of heirloom techniques. There would be no book if you had not encouraged me. Thank you for your blessings.

To my students, who allow me to influence them and in return allow me to learn from them.

My sincere gratitude to all of the fine, talented editors and photographers at C&T Publishing. Your commitment to my vision of this project deserves much praise.

preface

Upon attending my first hand-stitched silk ribbon design class a number of years ago, I immediately fell in love with the art. I planned all the lovely projects that I wanted to complete. There was only one problem: I was not enthusiastic about doing these projects by hand. Although I am successful with handwork, I found the challenge of executing the technique by machine to be very exciting.

After gathering all of the information I could find on machine technique, I returned to my sewing room with an armful of books and ribbon and began to teach myself ribbon design. I was not as pleased with the results as I had expected. The ribbons seemed to lie flat and look boxy against the fabric. Since the stitching did not appear as appealing as my handwork, my projects were put on hold. I needed more information.

I then began to think of the ribbon creations in geometric terms. By applying tension to the ribbon and holding it at specific angles, I could achieve different results. I deliberately planned the routing for each stitch throughout a design, instead of just dragging the ribbon around the needle and tacking it down. The ribbon flowers now seemed to blossom from the fabric as I developed a hand-stitched look.

It's about time! What's that about? Well, I have had the pleasure of teaching my angular technique to students across the country. For simplicity of instruction, I relate the angles to the hours of the traditional clock (heaven help the digital generations). "Hold the ribbon to 4 o'clock" or "Stitch in the direction of 2 o'clock." The directions are simple, and the students love the results. It is at their request that I have created this "timely" book detailing my instructions.

it's about time!

introduction

This step-by-step manual is designed to instruct new students of ribbon embroidery created by machine. Veterans of the technique will discover tips for improving their skills.

Each section is carefully detailed to provide the maximum information available. The book is basically written just as I would give one of my classes, and the assumption is that this is the first time you are being introduced to the technique. How to hold the ribbon, which direction to stitch, how far you should stitch, and when you might use a certain tool are just some of the topics addressed in this book.

A photograph taken from the sewer's point of view accompanies each step. The beginning of each lesson includes a photo of the finished stitch and a brief description, including suggested colors, ribbon sizes, and textures.

Eager as you are to begin stitching, take some time to read through this book first. It is packed with tips to make this art fun and easy. Knowing your goals will always lead to success.

Included at the back of this book is an appendix with free-motion exercises and patterns to play and practice with. You can also combine these exercises to create your own unique designs.

Relax. Have fun. And, as the book encourages, be creative!

tools, notions, and supplies

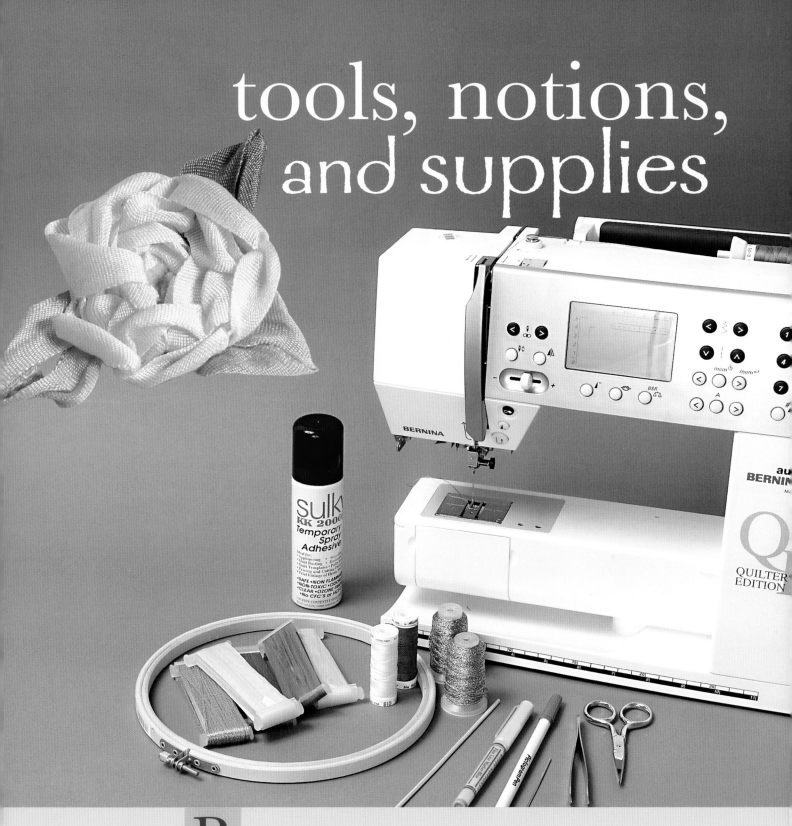

R eading the following information is definitely not as exciting as getting to the lessons and beginning to stitch, but don't set the cart before the horse. Please consider this chapter to be your first lesson; read it carefully as you assemble the items necessary to produce the best stitching possible.

Sewing Machines

You do not need a fancy machine for this work. The only stitch required is a straight stitch, which all machines have. I have even used my grandmother's treadle machine and achieved great results. Of course, the more stitch control available on the machine, the easier it will be for you to create. A machine that has the ability to stop with the needle down in the fabric is an asset.

Fabrics

Virtually any fabric that you can hoop or adhere to a hoop will work. I have stitched on a variety of textures, from sheer georgette to quilted fabrics and polar fleece. This technique is particularly wonderful on lightweight fabrics used for wedding veils and heirloom work. Since the ribbon stitching remains on top of the fabric, only half as much ribbon is used as is used in hand-sewn ribbon embroidery, resulting in a lightweight decoration.

The fabric preparation remains the same as for any project. If the item is to be worn or eventually washed, prewash the fabric. If your finished project will eventually be dry-cleaned, you may want to process your fabric in the same manner first. In general, pretreatment for wallhangings or other home decorating projects is optional.

Tools and Notions

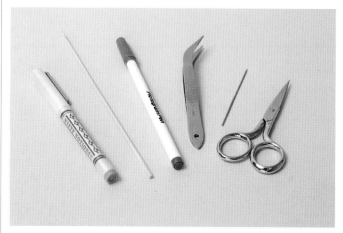

Essential tools

As in any craft, the correct tool for the job is extremely important. Following are the items that are required to produce pleasing results.

TWEEZERS

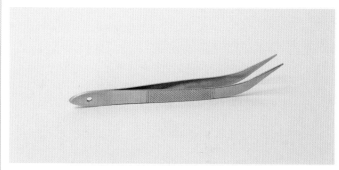

Prym-Dritz #918 serger-style tweezers

My favorite tweezers are a serger style by the Prym-Dritz Corporation, product number 918. It may sound silly to be so specific about this, but my students have come to class with such a variety of tweezers that even I wasn't aware there were so many available.

Sharp tweezers damage the silk ribbon by catching on the threads. Long, dental-style tweezers are difficult to hold and have serrated tips that injure the ribbon. Regular serger tweezers are great for thread-feeding a needle but lack the strength to control the ribbons.

Cosmetic tweezers have flat tips that cannot grab the ribbon successfully.

The Prym-Dritz #918 tweezers have a medium-length, well-balanced body for ease of holding. The blunt tips are fine enough to guide the ribbon without injuring the silk. When the tweezers are used upside down, "shovel" fashion, the long elbow provides a wide base that is necessary for executing specific techniques. These tweezers are usually available at national chain fabric stores.

SCISSORS

Small, sharp embroidery scissors are required for machine embroidery work. I achieve pleasing results using a straight 4″ knife-blade style. The size enables you to clip ribbons and threads quite close to the lowered needle at the end of the stitch. Larger or curved scissors leave excess ribbon tails, which may be difficult to conceal within the work.

MARKERS

Use your favorite form of pattern transfer or look in a fabric store's notions department for other suggestions. Most of the time, I use either a purple air-soluble or a blue washable marking pen. The latter requires just a spritz of water to make the drawn pattern disappear. If you wish to retain the drawing from an air-soluble pen to complete later, simply place it in an airtight, resealable bag.

WOODEN SKEWERS

Wooden kitchen skewers and bamboo collar-point turners are ideal for pushing the ribbon into place or for a technique called ruching (page 58). If you do not possess long fingernails, you will find these items invaluable. Should the machine needle come in contact with the wood tip, the needle will either slide to the side of the tip into the fabric or penetrate the tip of the skewer. In either case, a stitch has been created without breaking a needle. A damaged skewer tip is easily repaired by filing it with an emery board.

Instead of a wooden skewer, some people like to use a tool called a trolley needle. This sewing notion looks like a metal toothpick that extends from a band placed over the tip of the index finger. If you are comfortable with this item, use it. However, your chances of breaking a needle are much greater.

ADHESIVES AND STABILIZERS

Use temporary adhesives and water-soluble stabilizers to embroider hard-to-hoop items.

Spray adhesives, such as Sulky KK 2000 and 505 Spray and Fix, are invaluable in the sewing room. Both are temporary adhesives and are most effective when used in conjunction with a water-soluble stabilizer, such as Solvy by Sulky or OESD Badge Master. Use this combination to embroider hard-to-hoop items, such as collar points and cuffs, or on fabrics that can be damaged by hooping, such as velvet. Merely hoop the water-soluble stabilizer, spray it with adhesive, and smooth the fabric on top. After stitching, turn over the hoop and cut out the sewn portion, leaving a hole in the stabilizer. The remaining portion of the hooped stabilizer can be used repeatedly simply by spraying the top again and patching it with a small piece of water-soluble stabilizer.

NEEDLES

In general, use a needle that suits the fabric to be embellished. An 80/12 Universal is the needle size most frequently used. Smaller sizes or Sharps, used for fine fabrics such as batiste, may be used as necessary. Do not use a needle larger than size 90/14, as it will damage the silk ribbon. Always use a fresh needle when starting a project to avoid damaging ribbons and fabrics—small burrs create big problems!

THREAD

Monofilament, an invisible thread, is typically used for silk ribbon embroidery. It is available in smoke and clear colors. Use smoke for dark fabrics and clear for light fabrics. I like Superior Threads MonoPoly, Sulky Premier Invisible Polyester Monofilament, and Wonder Invisible Thread by YLI. All three are strong and resist breakage. These quality threads are thinner than generic craft types of invisible thread. Since the preferred threads are soft and pliable, your sewing machines will appreciate them and reward you with good stitch results.

For most types of designing, place the thread in the usual manner in both the upper thread guides and the bobbin area. If you are constructing a garment, you may wish to fill the bobbin with Bottom Line Thread from Superior or Lingerie and Bobbin Thread from YLI. These very strong synthetic threads feel soft next to the skin.

HOOPS

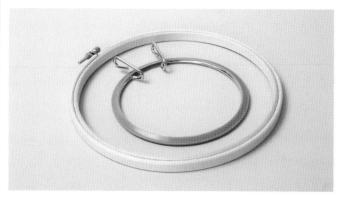

Hoops are essential tools in ribbon embroidery.

An 8″ embroidery hoop is usually a good size to use, as it allows most designs to be completed without rehooping. It also fits nicely under the arm of the sewing machine when you twirl the hoop to create certain stitches. A larger hoop may not pass as easily through this area.

Wooden hoops usually hold the fabric tauter than do spring-style hoops. However, even a wooden hoop will loosen over time. It is very difficult to stitch on fabric that bounces because it is loose in the hoop. To avoid loose fabric, wrap a wooden hoop with ½″-wide grosgrain ribbon: first, glue a strip of ribbon along the exterior edge of the inner hoop and then glue and wrap another length of ribbon around the outer hoop. This technique also prevents thinner fabrics from getting hoop burns and splitting fibers.

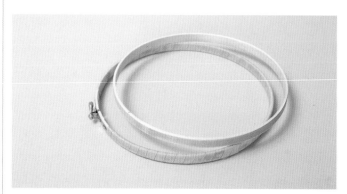

Grosgrain ribbon helps keep fabric taught.

Spring-style hoops are valuable when working on fragile fabrics. Designs created on these fabrics are usually quite small, and the smooth finish of this tool will protect the fabric. For fragile fabrics, I find a 5″ hoop works satisfactorily.

SNAG REPAIR TOOL

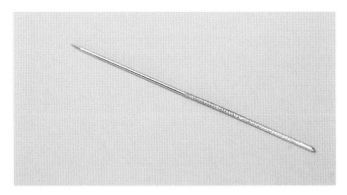

The snag repair tool's original purpose is to hide pulled threads in knits. It looks like a needle, but the upper half of the shaft is serrated. When the point of the tool is inserted into fabric, the serrations grab the loose thread or ribbon and pull it to the back of the piece.

Ribbons

Ribbons are available in a variety of styles.

SILK

Pure silk ribbon, as opposed to a silk blend, has a drapability that allows ease of manipulation. When ribbons move well, the designer can be more creative in stylizing realistic-looking flowers. Fine-quality ribbons are available from Superior Threads, as well as from YLI.

Ribbons are available in the following sizes (widths): 2mm, 3.5–4mm, 7mm, 13mm, and 32mm. The two largest sizes are the least popular for handwork, because their widths prohibit them from being drawn through fabrics. However, in manipulated machine work, they can be used on the fabric surface quite comfortably and artistically. In addition, 3.5mm and 4mm ribbons are similar enough in size that they can be used interchangeably.

Do not overlook the beautiful hand-dyed variegated silk ribbons. They will add vibrancy and a look of reality to any silk flower. They are available in sizes up to 13mm, are quite soft, and drape well. Dyed ribbons created at home, although very appealing and less expensive, tend to be stiff and may be difficult to use.

WOVEN EDGE

Tightly woven ribbons are not appropriate for most machine ribbon artistry; however, they make delightful loops and fold nicely into points. Lightweight or open weaves, as long as they are flexible, may help you achieve some interesting gathered designs.

Beads and Other Fiber Options

Whenever possible, I like to introduce beads and other fibers into my artwork. Consider using pearls and sequins, or add contrast with fancy yarns and decorator threads. Decorator threads are fancy, heavier-weight threads that will not fit through the eye of a needle. They are often used in the loopers of sergers or are couched (stitched) onto fabric with a cording presser foot. Scrapbook and yarn stores are good sources for coordinated fiber packs, charms, and buttons that you can incorporate into your work.

Specialty threads supply a creative touch.

There are many fiber options available to include in your creative palette. Explore the fiber and thread racks in specialty shops to discover all the surprises available to you.

Superior Threads

Razzle Dazzle

Jazz up your bouquets with French knots and loop flowers created with this full-bodied, dazzling thread.

Halo

This metallized decorative thread will add pizzazz to swirly chain-stitched stems.

Polyarn

The woolly texture of this thread adds a lot of interest to background stems, or try adding it to chains to fill in shapes like baskets.

YLI

Pearl Crown Rayon

Here is a shiny, twisted thread that becomes quite beautiful when couched as an outline of a stem. It also makes great loops or French knots.

Monet

This is a wonderful blend of wool and acrylic. One of my favorite ways to use this product is to combine four strands of a light brown Monet with a single strand of brown Pearl Crown Rayon for a wonderful, woody-looking branch.

Candlelight

This exciting thread contains strands of sparkle. Make a statement by combining lime green Candlelight with a forest green Pearl Crown Rayon to make leaves and French-knotted centers for poinsettias.

Spark Organdy

Here is a glittery, transparent ribbon that makes beautiful sparkling flower petals and adds another choice to the group of textures.

1000-Denier Silk Thread

This 100% pure filament silk is excellent to use in silk ribbon embroidery. Use it to create airy wisps and outlines with stem stitches.

Madeira

Glamour

These threads contain strands of sparkling metallic fibers intertwined with a colored thread.

Reflector

This 3mm ribbon is available only in silver. It is a shimmery knit braid made of the same material as street surface reflectors.

on your mark, get set

You wouldn't run a marathon without lots of preparation and training. Understanding your machine, tools, and techniques is just as important. Proper hooping of fabric guarantees a tight palette, which results in good stitch control. Repetitive sequencing of machine setup will become second nature. Embrace the tips on handling and cutting the ribbon. These procedures are tried and true and will ensure faultless stitches—a real confidence builder.

Hooping

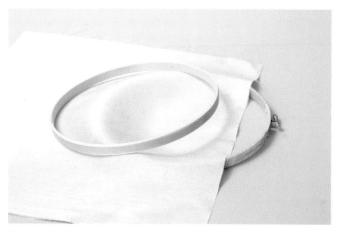

The outer hoop is beneath the fabric.

 *tip*

> You'll notice that this hooping method is the **reverse** of the hand-stitching method. For free-motion stitching, the fabric must remain flat against the sewing surface for proper stitch control.

1. Assemble the following layers on a table. *Do not do this on your lap.*

   Bottom: Outer hoop ring

   Middle: Fabric

   Top: Inside hoop ring

2. Push all the layers together; the hooped fabric will resemble a shallow bowl. Tighten the hooped fabric around the edges with a few firm tugs on the excess fabric.

3. Tighten the screw to secure the fabric. Test the fabric with a finger snap; it should sound like a drum. If the fabric loosens during sewing, tighten it again. Be aware that some fabric will loosen frequently as you work; stop and tighten as needed.

Machine Setup

Steps 1–6 apply to all sewing machines.

1. **Remove the presser foot.** Snap-on presser feet have a removable shank, or "ankle." Consult your machine's manual for specific instructions. In most cases, a small screw is all that holds the shank in place.

2. **Insert a new needle.** (80/12 for most projects; see Needles, page 10)

3. **Lower the feed dogs.** Refer to your machine's manual, if necessary. If your machine does not have this option, you can achieve the same result by covering your feed dogs with a thin sheet of paper or plastic. Tape it in place to provide a smooth surface for the hoop to glide on. Punch a small hole in the covering to allow the needle to pass through.

4. **Wind a bobbin with monofilament or bobbin thread** (see Thread, page 10). Monofilament thread goes a long way because it is quite thin. Wind the bobbin only one-third to half full. To prevent stretching, wind monofilament slower than normal thread by applying less pressure on the foot control or by adjusting the motor speed to one-half power.

Note: For garment embellishment, wind a full bobbin of Bottom Line by Superior or Lingerie and Bobbin Thread by YLI.

5. **Thread the machine with monofilament thread** (see Thread, page 10). Select clear for most applications or smoke for dark to black backgrounds.

6. **Lower the upper thread tension one level.**

Newer sewing machines have additional features that assist in creating ribbon artistry. Check the list below to see if any options apply to your machine.

Motor speed selection: Set this to half speed to deter "leadfoot" sewing.

Needle-stop up/down function: Select this option (usually by the push of a button) to ensure that the needle stops in a down position after each stitch.

Needle-stop up/down foot control: Check your owner's manual if you are not sure whether your machine has this highly desirable feature. A quick tap of your foot on the control allows you to raise or lower the needle without using your hands. You'll need to practice a bit, but this soon becomes second nature.

Presser foot lifter: This rod projects from the front of some machines, extending down next to the right knee. A simple push of the knee raises the presser foot, thus disengaging the upper tension. This mechanism enables you to move your hoop from one area to another without taking your hands off the work to raise the presser foot.

Extension table: If you have purchased one or have one that came with your machine, use it. This item gives a larger sewing surface, thus keeping the corner of the free arm from poking into the stretched fabric and loosening it from the hoop. This table is not necessary if your machine is already inserted into a cabinet for support.

Free-Motion Stitching

In this style of sewing, you guide the fabric. Set up your machine as described on page 14. Because the feed dogs are disengaged, the machine no longer advances the fabric for you. Typically, a darning or quilting foot is used to protect the loose fabric from bouncing during stitching. For our purpose, a presser foot is not necessary, because you hoop the fabric to protect it from bouncing under the needle.

I think that free-motion designing is great fun—it's simple to do and can be quite relaxing. Think of it as drawing by moving the paper instead of the pencil. Imagine the pencil suspended in the air as you slide

the paper around below it to create a design. Simply substitute the needle for the pencil and your hooped fabric for the paper. Use contrasting thread in the top and bobbin if you want your stitches to be noticed. Or use a matching thread if you want to hide them.

See Free-Motion Exercises (page 61) for designs to learn this technique. Practice stitching until you're comfortable guiding the hoop.

Notice the position of the hands in the photo. Your hands will remain in this position as you move the hoop sideways, up and down, or in swirling loops. The secret is to *never turn the hoop.* Keep a light contact touch on the sides of the hoop as you guide it. A death grip on the hoop will prohibit you from moving the hoop effectively.

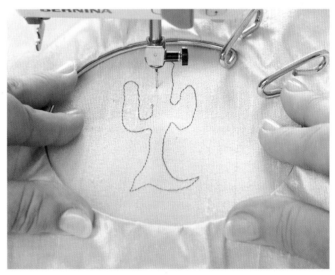

Keep a light touch on the hoop.

Use the straight stitch to get acquainted with the technique. Later, with practice, you'll want to try a zigzag stitch for a different look. Maintain a smooth speed while stitching and don't stitch too slowly; a regular sewing speed is fine. Each time you stop sewing, remove your foot from the pedal; this ensures that you will not accidentally stitch at an inappropriate time.

TAKING THE FIRST STITCH

1. After placing your hooped fabric under the needle, lower the machine's presser foot. If you don't do this, you'll create nests of thread under the hoop. The advantage of these nests is that you will not have to buy stuffing for pillows. The disadvantage is that you won't be able to remove the hoop from the machine. *I hope I've made my point.*

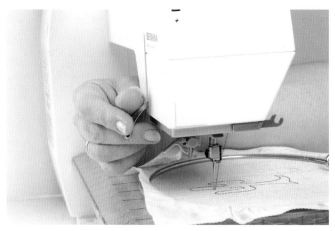

Always lower the presser foot.

2. The goal for the first stitch is to pull the bobbin thread up to the top of the hooped fabric. Use the handwheel to take 1 stitch into and out of the fabric to engage the lower thread. If you pull on the upper thread tail at this point, the lower thread will come along.

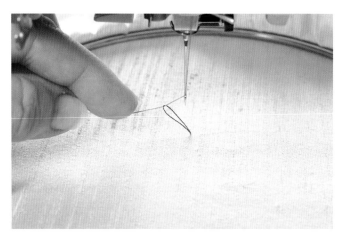

Pull the bobbin thread to the top of the fabric.

3. Hold the upper and lower thread tails aside; do not let them slip from your hands as you free-motion stitch a couple of tiny circles. This is called securing, or tacking, the stitch. Securing is important when using monofilament thread because the thread is so thin and can easily dislodge from the fabric. Take at least 10 little stitches to secure the thread.

Secure the thread.

4. Hold the ribbon as close to its tip as possible, exposing only a bit of it between your thumb and index finger. Squeeze the ribbon edges together with the tweezers and remove the ribbon from your grip. When using a wider ribbon, hold the ribbon in the same way, but use the tweezers to gather each edge to the center, making the tip narrower and easier to grab.

Hold the ribbon tip between thumb and index fingers.

Squeeze the ribbon edges together with tweezers.

5. You are now ready to attach the ribbon to the fabric. Gather the end of the ribbon with the tweezers. Support the ribbon between the tweezers with your left thumb and index finger as you slightly push the ribbon tip to the needle base. The tension on the ribbon at the needle should create a tiny V. Stitch across the gather. Your first stitch will pop off the fabric instead of just lying there. This is the beginning of a handmade look.

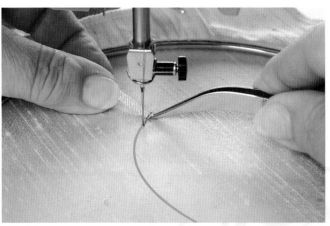

Secure the ribbon.

 *tip*

Some machine embroidery techniques begin by attaching the middle of the ribbon rather than the tip. Simply find the center of the ribbon length, push it up to the needle, and take a few tacking stitches to secure it in place.

it's about "time"

ENDING THE STITCH

1. Secure the end of the stitches as well as you did in the beginning. You don't want to run the risk of the stitches coming loose.

2. Trim or cut the ribbon away from the stitching. Keep in mind that you are using "invisible" thread—hard to see; easy to cut. Approach the ribbon with scissors open. Position the ribbon between the blades and slide the scissors toward the needle (which is in the down position). The thread is at the front of the needle, but the scissors are against the side, so there will be no damage to the thread. Close the very tip of the scissors to snip the ribbon.

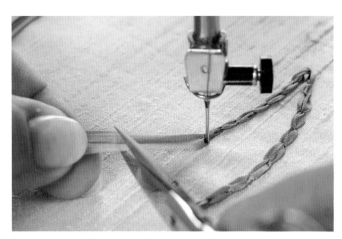

Approach the ribbon with scissors open.

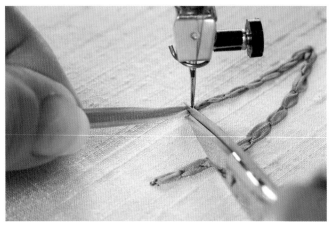

Snip the ribbon close to the needle.

Why am I so specific? You want your work to look like hand stitching. The ribbons will be cut clean, and you won't need to thread your needle so often.

tips and hints

Remembering these tips will prevent common problems.

- All stitches begin and end with the needle embedded in the fabric.

- Always take a few securing stitches at the beginning and end of a ribbon stitch.

- Remove your foot from the foot control when you are not stitching.

- Keep the fabric taut in the hoop at all times.

- Remember to keep the presser foot lever down, since there is no foot on the shank to visually remind you.

- It is not necessary to clip trailing threads (threads that extend from one design to another) until you finish the project. I remove them only when they get in the way or affect the look of the design. Seldom will I clip threads on the back of a project. Keeping the back threads intact secures the design.

- Although you may feel that it is necessary to constantly have a hold on the ribbon, keep in mind that the stitching direction and couching create the stitch. Sometimes it will be advantageous to let the ribbon rest as you stitch to the next tacking point. The ribbon will remain fresh looking and less wrinkled.

- Pay attention to the finger placements in the lesson photographs. When things don't look quite right with your work, improper finger placement could be the problem.

- Remember that it is the gathering of the ribbon at the front of the needle that duplicates the dimensional appearance of hand-stitched work.

chain stitches

The chain stitch is likely the most commonly used stitch for creating stems. It has wide appeal because it can be varied so easily. The stem width is controlled by the amount of tension applied to the ribbon. Try stitching curves and loops with this technique and you will soon be able to use it for creating monograms. For a different look, combine a decorator thread with a silk ribbon and then stitch the chain with both.

Commonly used silk ribbon: 2mm, 3.5–4mm, or 7mm

Variations: 1000-denier silk thread, needlepoint yarns, or any decorative threads suitable for couching

Ribbon length: 2 times the total length of the stems plus 2″

Note: Contrasting thread is used in photographs to emphasize stitches. Use an invisible thread to hide stitches in finished projects (see Thread, page 10).

Single Chain Stem

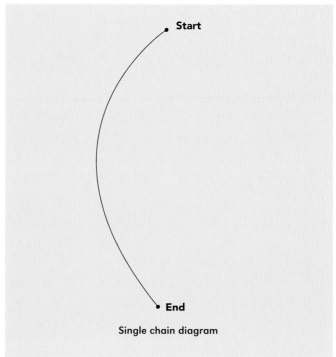

Single chain diagram

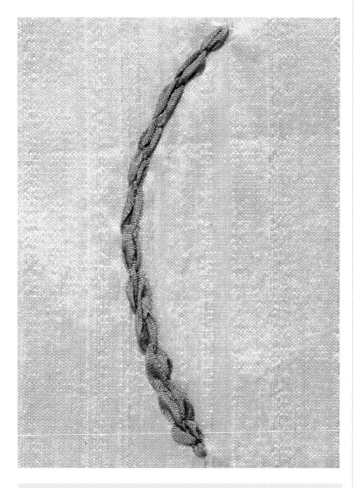

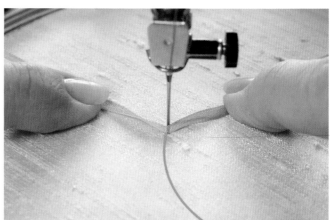

1. Draw the single chain diagram on your hooped fabric.

2. Choose a 9″ length of 3.5–4mm silk ribbon.

3. Starting at the tip of the drawn stem, secure the thread, stopping with the needle inserted in the fabric. Find the center point of the ribbon length and place the center snugly at the base of the needle. Lightly push the ribbon toward the needle with both index fingers; this motion will create a gather. Take a few stitches in place to attach the ribbon to the fabric.

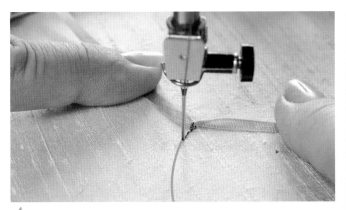

4. Move the hoop away from you as you stitch in the direction of 6 o'clock, approximately ¼″ down the stem line.

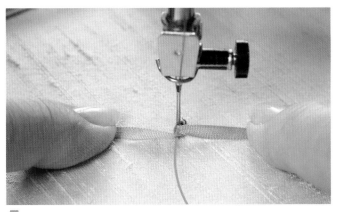

5. Crisscross the ribbon tails in front of the needle. Gently pull the ribbon sections to 9 o'clock and 3 o'clock with your index fingers. This movement applies a bit of tension to the ribbon at the needle, allowing the stitch to acquire a lofty appearance when it is completed.

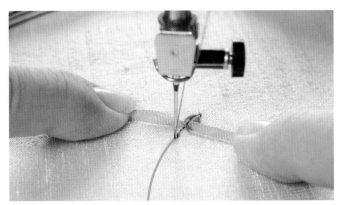

6. Stitch across the positioned ribbon and continue stitching on the stem line another ¼″.

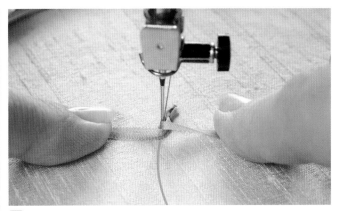

7. Repeat Steps 5 and 6 until the stem is completed. Be consistent with the direction in which the ribbons cross.

tip

The ribbon may be crossed left over right or right over left. It is your choice; just be consistent for a uniform look.

8. To end the stem, overlap the 2 ribbon tails and hold them in place with your fingertips. Move the hoop from side to side, stitching the ribbon in place. Cut away the excess ribbon (see page 18).

tip

The Snag Repair Tool

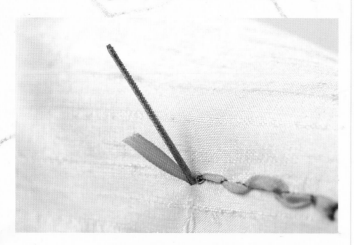

Insert tool from top and pull underneath fabric.

This handy gadget will help hide unwanted ribbon ends.
Insert the sharp end of the tool close to the end of your
stitching. As the serrated end of the tool enters the
fabric, make sure the ribbon contacts the tool. The
ribbon will be dragged to the back of the fabric.

Chain Stem
With Offshoot

1. Draw the offshoot diagram on your hooped fabric.

2. Choose a 12″ length of 3.5–4mm silk ribbon.

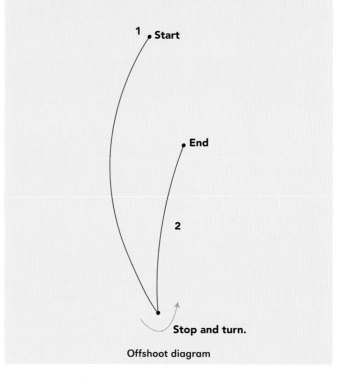

1 • **Start**

• **End**

2

Stop and turn.

Offshoot diagram

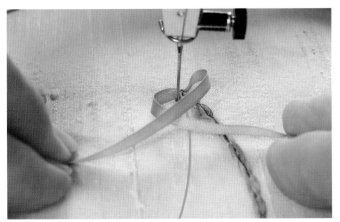

3. Create Stem 1 (follow Steps 3–7 of Single Chain Stem, page 20). End with the needle down at the junction of Stem 1 and Stem 2. Rotate the hoop so the route of Stem 2 is facing you, at 6 o'clock. Separate the loose ribbon tails.

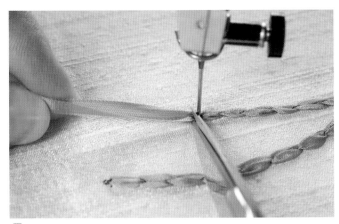

4. Crisscross the ribbons in front of the needle and continue chaining to the end of Stem 2.

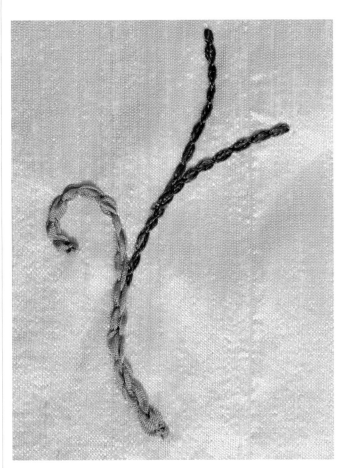

5. Tack across the end of the chain and then clip close to the needle to complete the stitches.

Multibranches and Blending Textures

Combining branches and textures will occur frequently, as most designs consist of more than one floral stem. Use the following rule of thumb to determine the sequence of layering: start at the bottom and work up (in other words, work from the background to the foreground). If you wish to indicate new growth on the same stem, use a lighter-weight ribbon or couching thread.

1. Draw the multibranch diagram on your hooped fabric.

2. Choose a 5″ length of 1000-denier silk thread for Stem 1 and a 5″ length for Stem 2. Choose an 8″ length of 3.5–4mm ribbon for Stem 3.

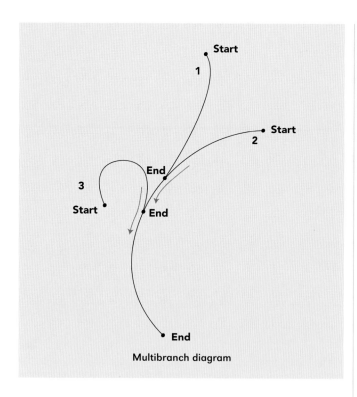

Multibranch diagram

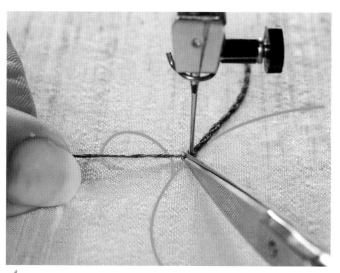

4. Tack the silk thread securely at the junction of Stem 2. Clip the thread tails very close to the embedded needle.

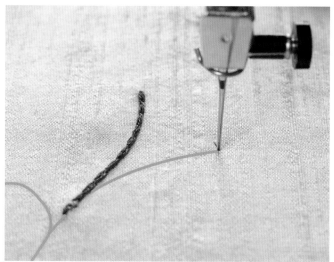

5. To move to the tip of Stem 2, raise the needle and release the thread tension (lift the presser foot). Do not cut the monofilament thread; instead, drag it to the next location by sliding the hoop. Lower the needle into the fabric at the tip of Stem 2. Drop the presser foot lever and take a few tacking stitches before beginning this new chain of stitches.

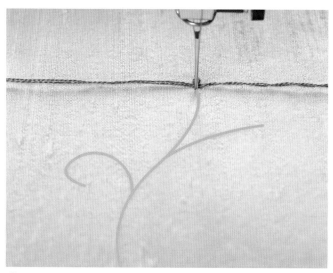

3. Secure the monofilament thread and then attach the center point of the silk thread to the fabric at the tip of Stem 1 (see Step 3, Single Chain Stem, page 20). Because the silk thread is thinner than ribbon, create the chains by crossing the thread every ⅛″ instead of every ¼″.

6. Attach the silk thread and chain stitch to the junction of Stem 3. As before, tack, clip, and drag the monofilament thread to the tip of Stem 3. *[Note: I have repeated dragging instructions for the ending and beginning of a new stitch only to reinforce the importance of securing the thread in the fabric. If this is not properly done, the ribbons will loosen from the fabric when the dragged threads are clipped or the fabric is washed.]*

7. Rotate the hoop so the stitching route is facing you. Attach the 3.5–4mm silk ribbon and begin to chain around the curve. As each stitch is completed, rotate the hoop a little so your route always remains directly in front of you at the 6-o'clock position.

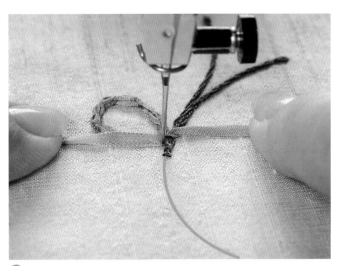

8. Continue stitching over the junction of Stem 2 to the end of Stem 3.

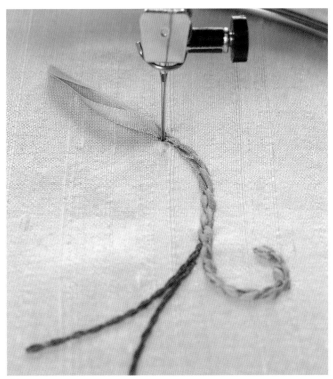

9. Secure and clip the ribbon to finish the stem. If no other design or stitching is intended to cover the clipped end, you may wish to use the snag repair tool to draw any excess ribbon ends to the back of the fabric. *[Note: The image view is rotated to show stitch detail.]*

stem stitches

Other styles of stem stitches are useful for filling in areas where you don't want a flower but still desire some coverage. The curled stem closely resembles the hand-sewn whipstitch. With practice, this stitch can become quite slender. Normally this technique is executed in greens for flower stems, but you might consider using browns and rusts to create branches for such plants as salt cedar and redbud.

The flipped or twisted stem is fun to use. Created with a variety of ribbons or threads, this stem is useful for representing a nubby type of stem or branch. I especially like to use a thickly textured thread called bouclé when working this stem, because the thread itself is nubby and adds to the textured look of the finished design.

Commonly used silk ribbon: 2mm, 3.5–4mm, or 7mm

Variations: needlepoint yarns, bouclé, or any decorative thread suitable for couching

Ribbon length: total length of the stems plus 1″

Note: Contrasting thread is used in photographs to emphasize stitches. Use an invisible thread to hide stitches in finished projects (see Thread, page 10).

Curled Stem

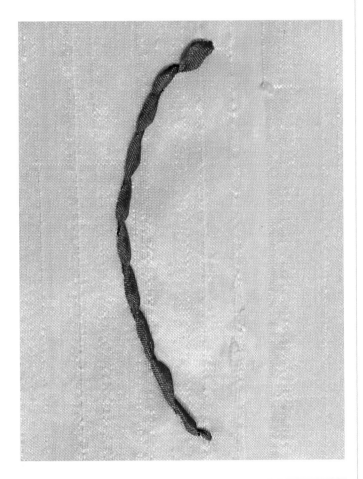

1. Draw a curved line approximately 3″–4″ long on your hooped fabric (see Single Chain Diagram, page 20). Make the line curve a couple times, if you wish.

2. Choose a 5″ length of 3.5–4mm silk ribbon.

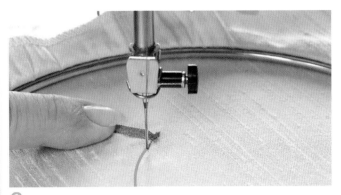

3. Secure the thread. Hold the ribbon to 9 o'clock with your left hand. Squeeze the edge with the tweezers. Tack the tip in place and continue to stitch ¼″ down the drawn stem.

4. Drag the ribbon across the front of the needle with your right hand. Pull it slightly to 3 o'clock and press it in place with your index finger, fairly close to the needle. The amount of tension on the ribbon at the needle will determine the width of the stem.

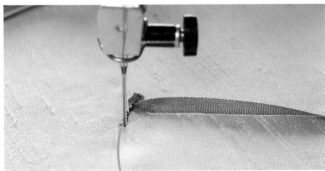

5. Stitch across the ribbon and down the stem about ¼″. [*Note: You may have stitched on the ribbon or jumped over the ribbon. It makes no difference, because the thread is holding the stitch in place. The result is the same.*]

6. Curl the ribbon from the back to the front of the needle (see Tip, below).

7. With your finger, apply tension on the ribbon as it is held to 3 o'clock. Again stitch ¼″ down the stem. Repeat Steps 6 and 7 to finish the stem.

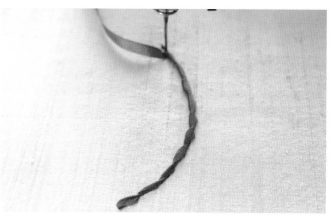

8. Secure the ribbon tails in place. The finished result is quite similar to a handmade whipstitch. *[Note: The image view is rotated to show stitch detail.]*

Flipped Stem

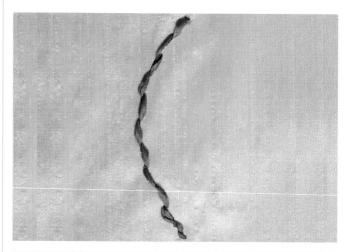

1. Draw a line approximately 3″–4″ long on your hooped fabric (see Single Chain Diagram, page 20). Make the line curve a couple of times, if you wish.

2. Choose a 5″ length of 3.5–4mm silk ribbon.

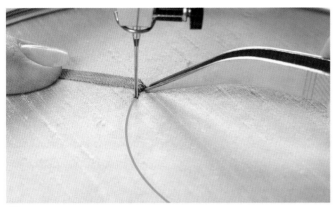

3. Secure the thread. As you hold the ribbon to 9 o'clock with your left hand, secure the ribbon tip and continue to stitch ¼" down the drawn stem.

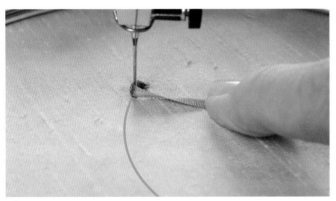

4. Drag the ribbon across the front of the needle with your right hand. Pull it slightly to 3 o'clock and press it in place with your index finger, fairly close to the needle. I find that I prefer a looser ribbon tension on this stitch.

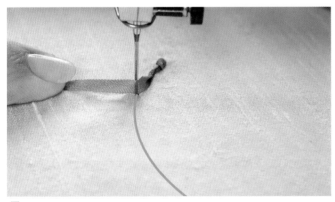

5. Stitch across the ribbon and ¼" down the drawn stem. Drag the ribbon across the front of the needle and press it to 9 o'clock with your left index finger.

6. Stitch down the stem again and flip the ribbon across the needle to the other side.

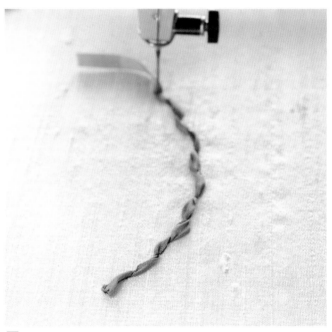

7. Continue this flip-and-stitch method until the stem is completed. Since each ribbon stitch rests on alternate sides of the drawn stem, this technique is quite suitable for creating branches—a great natural look! *[Note: The image view is rotated to show stitch detail.]*

loop flowers

Loops are fantastic for creating flowers that provide dimension and volume within your design. Keep in mind that when the loops or petals are not secured to the fabric at the edges, the loose ends may reveal the raw edges of previously stitched stems or leaves; so, be careful where you place them. Loops usually work well at the tips of stems or in the joints of branches and leaves.

Loop flowers are a style of fantasy flower. They can resemble violets, daisies, or mums. You are the designer—be creative! How do you assemble loops to stylize other flowers? Try using a multicolor silk ribbon to create loops placed next to each other along a spiraled line—this makes a great-looking dahlia.

In this lesson, you will learn to make two types of loops: freestyle and secured.

Commonly used silk ribbon: 3.5–4mm, 7mm, or 13mm (2mm is seldom used, but if it fits your needs, go for it!)

Variations: woven-edged ribbon, Spark Organdy

Ribbon length: multiply length needed per loop by number of loops (spokes) per flower, then add 2″

Note: The required amount of ribbon has a direct relationship to the width of the ribbon. The chart applies to a basic loop flower and allows you to calculate the needed amount of ribbon for various widths. As you create other designs, feel free to adjust and vary ribbon lengths as necessary.

Note: Contrasting thread is used in photographs to emphasize stitches. Use an invisible thread to hide stitches in finished projects (see Thread, page 10).

Ribbon Width	Loop Length	# of Loops per Flower	Length Needed per Loop	Plus 2″	Total Length
13mm	1″	X	Multiply X by 2″	Add 2″	= _____
7mm	³⁄₄″	X	Multiply X by 1½″	Add 2″	= _____
3.5–4mm	½″	X	Multiply X by 1″	Add 2″	= _____
2mm	¼″	X	Multiply X by ½″	Add 2″	= _____

Freestyle Loops

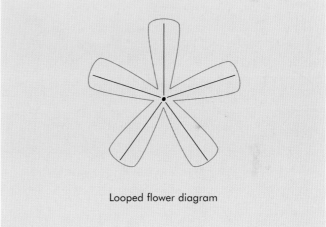

Looped flower diagram

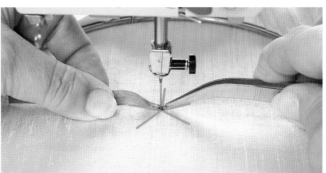

1. Draw a dot for the center of the flower on your hooped fabric. Draw 5 spokes around it, evenly spaced and each approximately ³⁄₄″ long.

2. Choose a 9½″ length of 7mm silk ribbon.

3. Secure the thread and ribbon tip to the center of the flower. Rotate the hoop so a spoke is positioned behind the needle at 12 o'clock.

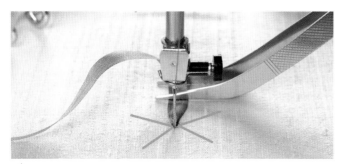

4. Hold the tweezers in your right hand, and turn upside down so they resemble a shovel. Hold the ribbon in your left hand and position it behind the needle in the direction of 12 o'clock. Slip the ribbon between the tweezers tips. Plant the tweezers firmly onto the fabric at the end of the spoke. This maneuver positions the length of the petal.

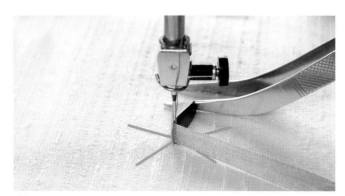

5. Pull the ribbon over the tweezers toward the front of the needle and gently pull the tail to rest at 4 o'clock.

6. Using your left index finger, press the ribbon tail tightly against the fabric an inch or so from the needle. Take a few tacking stitches in place on the ribbon.

tip

Do not move the hoop; just rotate it. This entire flower is created without moving the needle from the center of the flower.

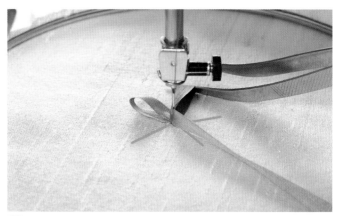

7. With the needle down, rotate the hoop to place the next spoke at 12 o'clock. Create another loop. Repeat to complete all 5 ribbon loops.

8. When all the loops have been made, secure them by sewing in a small circle over the excess ribbon at the center of the flower. Snip away the remaining ribbon and fluff the loops.

Secured Loops

1. Draw a dot for the center of the flower on your hooped fabric. Draw 5 spokes around it, evenly spaced and each approximately 3/4″ long (see Looped Flower Diagram, page 31).

2. Choose a 9½″ length of 7mm silk ribbon.

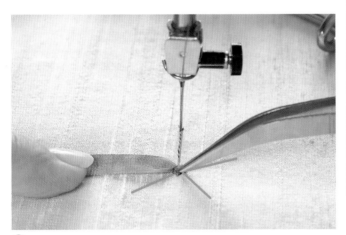

3. Secure the thread and ribbon tip to the center of the flower. Rotate the hoop so a spoke is positioned behind the needle at 12 o'clock. Move the hoop toward you as you stitch backward to the tip of the 12-o'clock spoke. Hold the ribbon at 9 o'clock.

4. Pull the ribbon toward 12 o'clock and let it lie flat next to the stitched line.

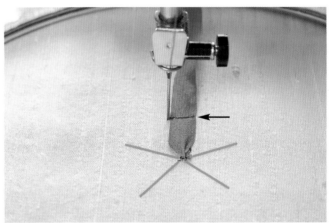

5. Stitch across the ribbon from right to left.

6. Stitch down the fabric back to the center of the flower. Another option, as shown here, is to raise the needle, raise the presser foot, and drag the needle back to the center of the flower. Drop the presser foot to begin stitching again. Either of these choices works well. Try them both and decide which you prefer.

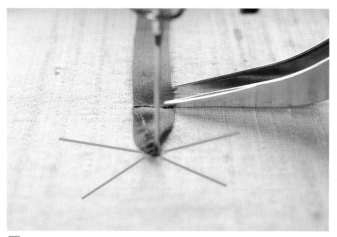

7. Place the tweezers, shovel style, just to the back of the line stitched across the ribbon.

8. Lift the ribbon over the tweezers and apply slight tension as you pull the ribbon in front of the needle to 4 o'clock. Tack the loop in place at the flower center. Using the tweezers in this method will give loft to the loop. If you do not use them and simply pull the ribbon around the front of the needle, the result will be a flat stitch. This may be your goal—again, you are the designer.

9. Repeat Steps 3–8 to create the remaining loops on the spokes. If the stitched guideline is not in the place you prefer, simply stitch over to relocate the needle to the desired position and continue with ribbon placement. The loop position is about $\frac{1}{8}''$ to the right of the stitching.

10. End the flower by stitching a small circle in the center of the loops. Clip away the remaining ribbon.

the lazy daisy

One of the most popular ribbon embroidery stitches is the lazy daisy. Does anyone know why it is called that? If you have an answer, let me know. It is a simple design. Perhaps the name indicates the ease with which this stitch is created, whether by hand or by machine. Depending on the width of the ribbon used, this stitch can be used to create a variety of posies that range in size from tiny violets to extravagant sunflowers. It is also perfect for the sweet daisy. Usually, this floral design consists of five or six petals surrounding the center.

Commonly used silk ribbon: 2mm, 3.5–4mm, or 7mm

Variations: decorative threads and yarns in single or multiples, Spark Organdy

Even though this stitch is called the lazy daisy, your ribbon color choice can turn it into other types of flowers. For instance, white or yellow makes a daisy, but lavender or blue makes a violet. Use 2mm ribbon to construct groups of tiny flowers and call it a stem of lilacs.

Ribbon length: multiply length needed per loop by number of loops (spokes) per flower, then add 2″

Note: The required amount of ribbon has a direct relationship to the width of the ribbon. The chart applies to a basic loop flower and allows you to calculate the needed amount of ribbon for various widths. As you create other designs, feel free to adjust and vary ribbon lengths as necessary.

Note: Contrasting thread is used in photographs to emphasize stitches. Use an invisible thread to hide stitches in finished projects (see Thread, page 10).

Ribbon Width	Loop Length	# of Loops per Flower	Length Needed per Loop	Plus 2″	Total Length
13mm	1″	X	Multiply X by 2″	Add 2″	= _____
7mm	3/4″	X	Multiply X by 1 1/2″	Add 2″	= _____
3.5–4mm	1/2″	X	Multiply X by 1″	Add 2″	= _____
2mm	1/4″	X	Multiply X by 1/2″	Add 2″	= _____

Lazy Daisy

1. Draw a dot for the center of the flower on your hooped fabric. Draw 6 spokes around it, evenly spaced and each approximately 1/2″ long.

2. Choose an 8″ length of 3.5–4mm silk ribbon.

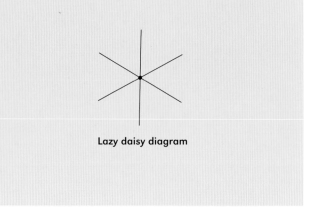

Lazy daisy diagram

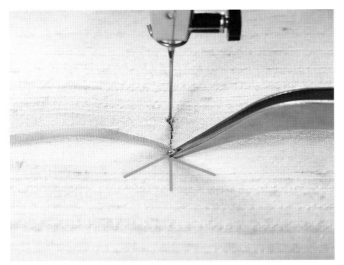

3. Secure the thread and tack the tip of the ribbon in place at the center of the flower. Rotate the hoop so a spoke is positioned behind the needle at 12 o'clock. Stitch backward to the tip of the 12-o'clock spoke, while holding the ribbon at 9 o'clock.

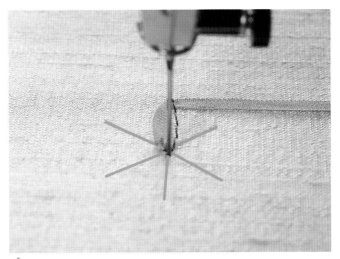

5. Take a single jump stitch backward over the standing ribbon. This will force the ribbon to lie down. If you have allowed enough slack in the ribbon, the left side of the petal should appear curved. Take a couple of tacking stitches in place.

4. Loosely wrap the ribbon around the back of the needle from the left side. Extend the ribbon to 3 o'clock. Hold the ribbon in place with your fingertip. The bend of the ribbon should stand at the back of the needle.

6. Stitch down from the just-secured petal tip, along the right side of the drawn spoke. End where you began, at the flower center.

7. Place the extended ribbon tail to the right side of the needle. Let it lie flat on the fabric. This will create the other side of the petal and will define its width.

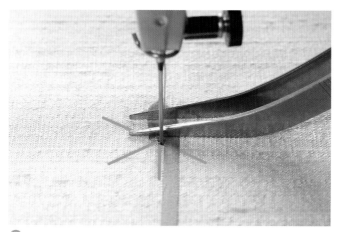

8. Firmly place the tweezers, shovel style, behind the needle on top of the ribbon. This will hold the width securely.

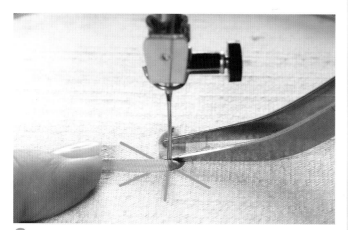

9. As you hold the tweezers in place, pull the ribbon tail to 9 o'clock. A gather will be made at the

needle. Tack the ribbon in place here. *[Note: The hoop will not move, because you are applying pressure with your left hand as well as with the tweezers.]*

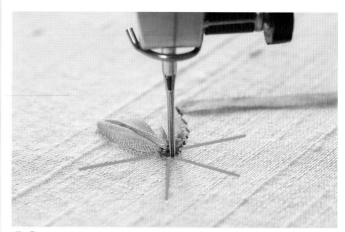

10. Follow Steps 3–9 to create the remaining loops on the spokes. Pay particular attention to correct placement as you manipulate the ribbon. The angles indicated in Steps 3–9 will produce perfect petals.

11. To end the flower, simply take a few tacking stitches at the center. When you have learned to make French knots (page 55), you may want to place a few in a contrasting color in the center of your flower.

the large leaf

A truly beautiful and graceful leaf provides the perfect backdrop for roses, pansies, and other single flowers that benefit from such fine framing. The formation of the large leaf stitch is loosely based on the lazy daisy stitch (page 36). This stitch looks best with 7mm and 13mm ribbons—my personal favorite is 7mm. As you become comfortable shaping this stitch, you can try a 3.5–4mm ribbon to back tiny single flowers. Variegated ribbons add depth and interest to the leaf's character. One of my favorite combinations is an ivory/light peach leaf behind a white open rose. I used this on a wedding dress, and the bride really loved it.

Commonly used silk ribbon: 3.5–4mm, 7mm, or 13mm

Variations: most woven ribbons—however, I do not recommend organdy, as it is transparent

Ribbon length: 4 times the *width* of the ribbon per leaf plus 2″

Note: Contrasting thread is used in photographs to emphasize stitches. Use an invisible thread to hide stitches in finished projects (see Thread, page 10).

Large Leaf

1. Draw the heart-shaped leaf diagram on your hooped fabric.

2. Choose a 4″ length of 7mm silk ribbon. As you gain experience with this stitch, you'll be able to begin with less ribbon.

Large heart-shaped leaf diagram

 *tip*

The length of the leaf should be slightly longer than twice the width of the ribbon. The length of a heart-shaped leaf is measured from the center of its rounded base to its pointed tip. A small dot in the center of the leaf indicates the half-length point.

For example, a 7mm ribbon would require a leaf designed approximately 15mm in length (or around 5/8″). Please do not get out your rulers. Just eyeball the size—that should do the trick.

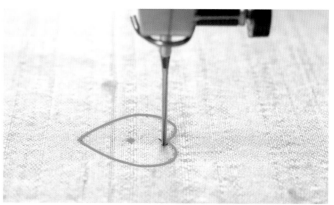

3. Turn the hoop so the tip of the leaf points to 9 o'clock.

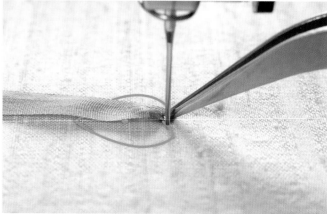

4. Secure the thread at the rounded base. Using tweezers, push the tip of the ribbon up to the front of the needle and tack it to the base of the leaf.

5. Rotate the hoop so the tip of the leaf points to you at the 6-o'clock position. *[Note: Steps 3–5 may seem trivial, but they are critical to the creation of the leaf's center vein.]*

6. Move the ribbon out of the way and stitch to the dot at the center of the leaf.

7. Position the ribbon so it lies flat down the center of the design. Curl it under at the front of the needle,

with the ribbon tail extending to the 3-o'clock position. Hold the tip of the curve in place with your wooden skewer. Notice how this step creates a miter.

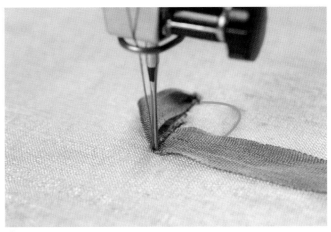

8. Continue stitching down the center of the leaf toward the leaf tip. Avoid stitching on the ribbon that is left of the center. Stop stitching about $^1/_{16}$″ before the edge of the ribbon. This maneuver creates a cute flip at the tip of the finished leaf. *[Note: This takes practice, but it is worth it. Image view is rotated to show stitch detail.]*

9. Do not handle the ribbon at this point. Stitch back to the point where the leaf began. Avoid stitching the finished half of the leaf.

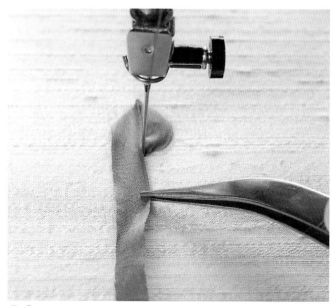

10. Lay the loose ribbon tail flat against the left side of the needle. This creates the other side of the leaf and defines its width.

12. A gather will be made at the needle; tack the ribbon in place here and then clip away the excess ribbon.

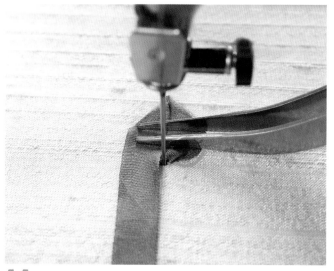

11. Place the tweezers, shovel style, firmly behind the needle on top of the ribbon. This holds the width of the leaf securely. While holding the tweezers in place, pull the ribbon tail across the front of the needle in the 3-o'clock direction.

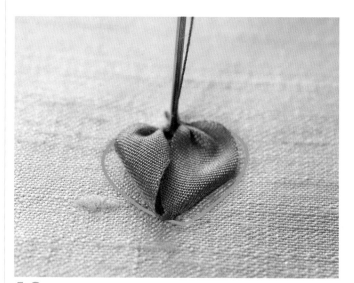

13. The tension created on the ribbon with the tacking stitch is enough to raise the ribbon off the fabric, giving a 3-dimensional appearance to the leaf.

the open rose

One of nature's most beautiful flowers is the rose. The closest hand embroidered duplication of this flower has been achieved by a stitch called the Web Rose, using the hand-stitched ribbon embroidery method. As machine embroiderers, we can create this stitch using a simple chain stitch worked in a spiral around a center bud.

The most successful flowers are created using 7mm or 13mm silk ribbon.

At first, your roses may look flat to you. Be patient—the flower's appearance will improve as you become looser with your work, thus creating more volume. Variegated ribbons can add realism to your floral creations. Use two different colors of ribbon, one on each side of the chain, for a special look. A pale yellow on one side and a light pink on the other will make a beautiful rose called Lovely Girl. Ah, but I digress to my days in the floral industry.

Commonly used silk ribbon: 3.5–4mm, 7mm, or 13mm

Variations: bias cuts of silk ribbon in the same widths as listed above

Ribbon length: 12″ per rose

Note: A 1″-wide rose will require 10″–12″ of 7mm ribbon. Your tension on the ribbon determines whether more or less is needed. If you run short, fold under and secure the ending ribbon, then tack on a new one.

Note: Contrasting thread is used in photographs to emphasize stitches. Use an invisible thread to hide stitches in finished projects (see Thread, page 10).

Open Rose

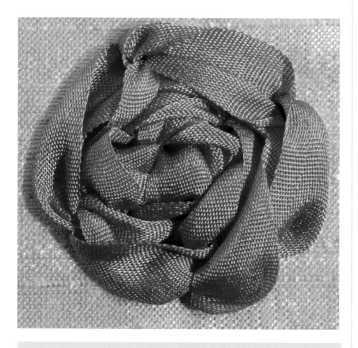

1. Draw the open rose diagram on your hooped fabric. The 3 dots should be placed where you wish the center of the rose to be on the fabric. The dots are spaced about ¼″ apart.

2. Choose a 12″ length of 7mm silk ribbon.

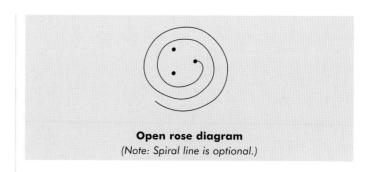

Open rose diagram
(Note: Spiral line is optional.)

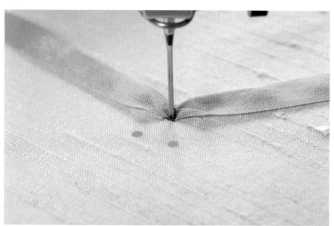

3. Insert the needle into the top dot and take a few tacking stitches to secure the thread. Find the center of the ribbon, give it a twist, and push the twist up against the needle. Tack it in place.

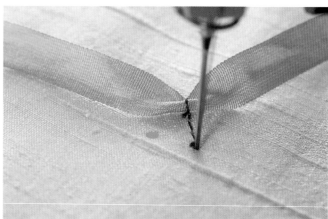

4. Holding the ribbon aside, stitch to the dot at the lower right.

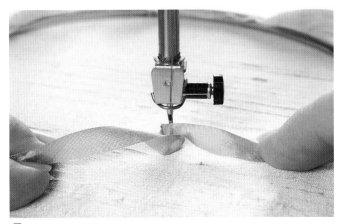

5. Cross the ribbon tails in front of the needle, left over right. This is important, as it creates loft when you stitch around the rose in a clockwise manner.

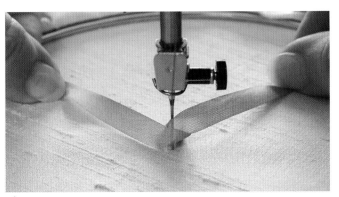

6. After you have crossed the ribbons, hold the tails at 10 o'clock and 2 o'clock to create proper tension at the needle.

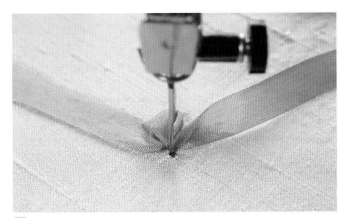

7. Take a single jump stitch across the crossed ribbon.

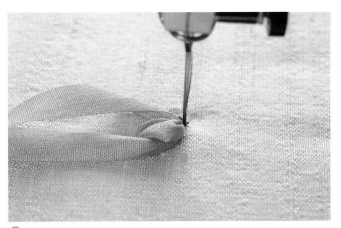

8. Rotate the hoop to expose the final dot in the 6-o'clock position.

9. Stitch to the final dot. [Note: The image view is rotated to show stitch detail.]

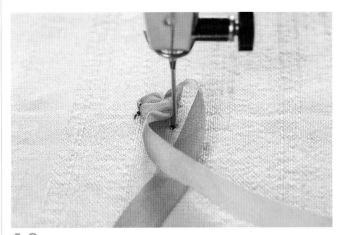

10. Bring the ribbons from the back to cross left over right in front of the needle. Hold the ribbon tails at 10 o'clock and 2 o'clock and make a jump stitch to tack in place. [Note: The image view is rotated to show stitch detail.]

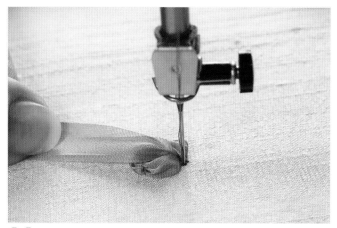

11. Hold the ribbons aside and stitch to the beginning dot.

12. As before, cross the ribbon tails and take a jump stitch to create the last of the 3 chains that make the center bud.

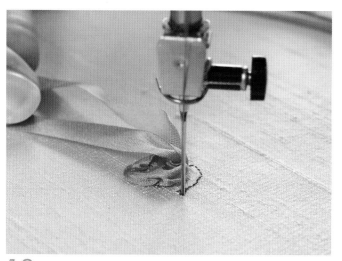

13. To make the outer petals, begin stitching in a spiral approximately $1/8''$ from the bud (or follow the optional drawn spiral line). Stitch approximately $1/2''$ around the bud before creating the next chain.

14. Rotate the hoop and apply tension to the ribbon by holding the ends to 10 o'clock and 2 o'clock for each chain stitch before making the jump stitch.

it's about "time"

15. Stop chaining when you have reached the desired size for your flower.

16. Using the tip of the tweezers, tuck the ribbon tail that is extending from the right side under a previously chained rose petal in front of the needle. [Note: Trim ribbon tails to a comfortable length if they are too long to tuck.]

17. Using a wooden skewer, pull back a petal from the previously created row to avoid stitching into it

and to expose the end of the tucked ribbon. Tack the tucked ribbon end to the fabric and then release the rose petal to cover the stitching.

18. Using the tweezers, grab the remaining ribbon tail. Pull it behind the needle to the right side. Then curl it across the front of the needle. Tuck and stitch the ribbon as in Step 17.

19. After the rose is complete, fluff it by squeezing it a couple of times to loosen any ribbons that may be confined by crossing threads.

the rosebud

A rosebud is simple in form yet intriguingly beautiful. It is amazing to see how quickly a luscious strip of ribbon becomes a realistic bud. Display a few on collars and cuffs or fill an embroidered basket with an array of these pretty petals. Hand-dyed ribbon makes this flower most appealing as you peer into the rolled center and notice darker edges spiraling inward.

For this technique, my favorite width of ribbon is 7mm, which produces a bud that measures almost ½″ in length with a graceful fold at the end of the stitch. With more practice, you can achieve a successful result with a 13mm ribbon. I don't recommend using a 3.5–4mm ribbon, as this width usually produces a boxy-looking bud.

Commonly used silk ribbon: for rosebud—7mm or 13mm; for calyx and stem—2mm or 3.5–4mm

Variations for rosebud: Spark Organdy and some loosely woven bridal ribbons

Ribbon length: for rosebud—2″–3″ per bud; for calyx refer to Lazy Daisy (page 36); for stem refer to Flipped Stem (page 28) for measurements

Note: Contrasting thread is used in photographs to emphasize stitches. Use an invisible thread to hide stitches in finished projects (see Thread, page 10).

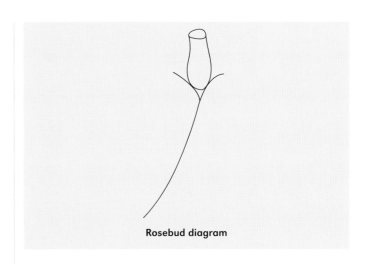

Rosebud diagram

Rosebud

1. Draw the ½″ rosebud diagram, including the stem and small side leaves, on your hooped fabric.

2. Choose a 3″ length of 7mm ribbon. As you gain experience with this stitch, you'll be able to use 2″ of ribbon and still have extra to trim away.

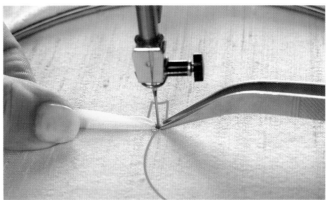

3. Secure the thread. Using tweezers and keeping the ribbon tail at the 9-o'clock position, attach the end of the ribbon to the bottom center of the bud.

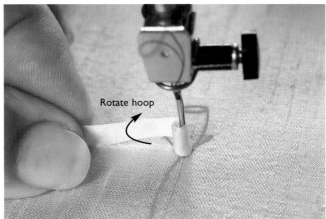

Rotate hoop

4. While holding the ribbon to the left, rotate the hoop clockwise. This motion will wrap the ribbon around the needle. Keep rotating the hoop to create 3 wraps.

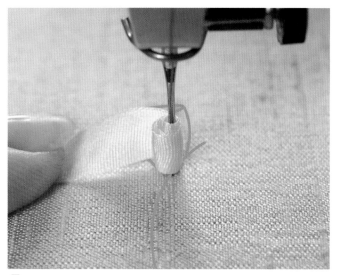

5. Place your left index finger on the ribbon tail at 9 o'clock, laying it flat against the fabric and preventing it from unwrapping. The ribbon cylinder should have a relaxed wrap around the needle. At this point, the stem should be directly below the needle and pointing toward you at the 6-o'clock position.

6. Turn the handwheel so the needle rises out of the ribbon cylinder.

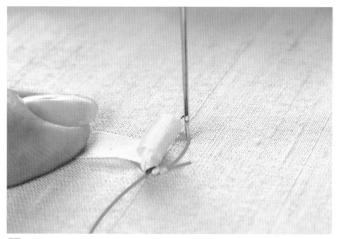

7. Continue turning the handwheel. As the needle lowers, slowly move the hoop toward you. This motion will cause the ribbon cylinder to lie down backward onto the fabric at 12 o'clock. [Note: The needle should enter the fabric at the tip of the cylinder only. Image view is rotated to show stitch detail.]

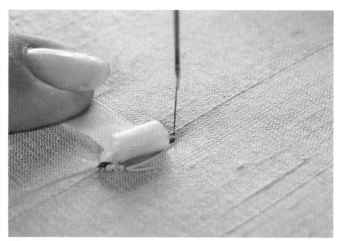

8. Take a few tacking stitches to hold the cylinder in place. If necessary, pull the bottom of the wrapped ribbon with tweezers to prevent it from being caught at the tip when tacking. [Note: The image view is rotated to show stitch detail.]

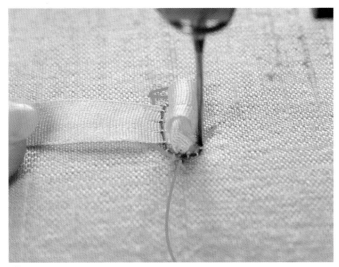

9. Stitch from the tip of the cylinder downward along the left side across the extended ribbon tail. Continue stitching around the bottom of the cylinder and slightly up the right side, stopping at 4 o'clock. The stitching will resemble a backward "J."

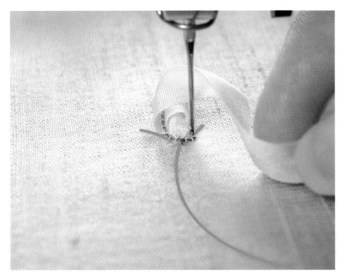

10. Flip the ribbon tail behind the needle from the left side over to the right, placing it at 3 o'clock across the cylinder.

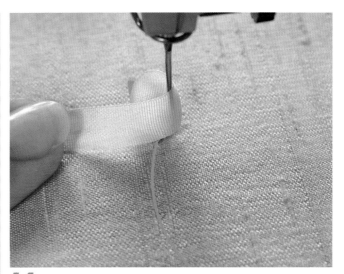

11. Pull the ribbon tail from the right, curling the ribbon across the front of the needle, perpendicular to the fabric so the top edge faces up toward you. End the wrap at 9 o'clock. Hold the ribbon securely against the fabric with your left index finger about ¹/₂″ from the needle. As you can see, the ribbon will stand loosely against the right side of the needle, providing the support the ribbon requires for the final stitch.

12. Before taking the next stitch, check the tension of the ribbon against the needle. If it is too tight, you won't get the pretty fold. Jump stitch over the wrapped ribbon with 1 or 2 short stitches directed to 4 o'clock. Tack in place.

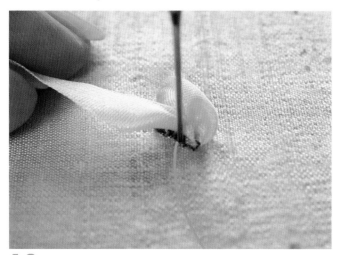

13. Pull the ribbon tail back and out of the way. Stitch across the fabric from the tacking point to the bottom center of the bud. Secure the ribbon tail against the back of the needle and tack in place. Clip the remaining ribbon. The ending ribbon tail will be hidden when you add the calyx and stem.

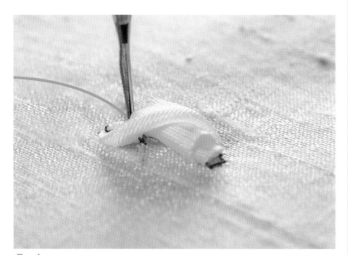

14. Voilà—the rosebud! Rotate the hoop to admire your work. Do not cut the thread before beginning the calyx and stem. *[Note: The image view is rotated to show stitch detail.]*

Rosebud Calyx and Stem

1. Choose a 6˝ length of 3.5–4mm silk ribbon. Attach the ribbon end to the base of the rosebud.

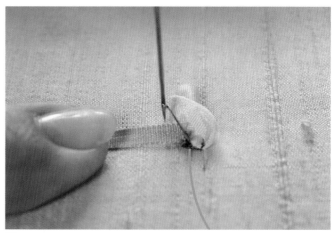

2. Create a small lazy daisy stitch (page 36); this will be the calyx of the bud. Start stitching quite close against the bottom left side of the bud. Stitch to the tip of the short drawn line.

3. At the tip of the calyx leaf, wrap the ribbon from left to right behind the needle. Tack the ribbon in place at the tip and return the needle to the base of the rosebud. Tack the ribbon in place.

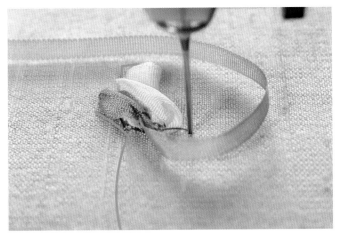

4. In the same manner, create the right calyx leaf, but instead wrap the loop right to left behind the needle. End the calyx where you began at the base of the rosebud. Tack the stitches in place, *but do not cut the ribbon.*

6. Stitch ¼″ down the stem line. Create a flipped stem stitch (see page 28) along the drawn stem line. Secure the ending stitches.

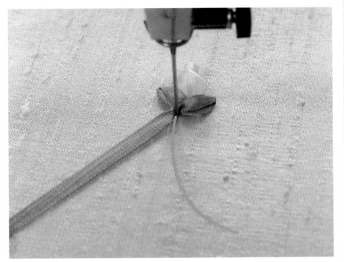

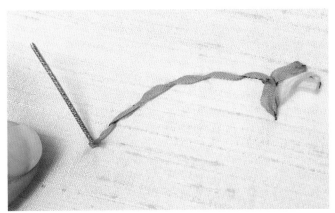

5. Wrap the calyx leaves snugly near the rosebud, so the bud will appear to be emerging from the calyx.

7. Clip the ribbon and use the snag repair tool to pull any excess ribbon to the back of the fabric.

it's about "time"

the french knot

Practice—and lots of it—makes perfect on these tricky little stitches. These are definitely easier to accomplish by hand but are not impossible by machine. The wrap and tension will be your keys to success. Individual knots indicate buds. Try clustering them in various sizes to create wisteria or grapes. Using a variegated ribbon adds a touch of realism, as well as depth, to the design.

These stitches can be achieved using almost any width of ribbon. For most treatments, you'll be successful using a 3.5–4mm or 7mm silk ribbon; however, I recall embellishing a wedding gown with puffy balls using 13mm ribbon.

Commonly used silk ribbon: 2mm, 3.5–4mm, 7mm, or 13mm

Variations: decorator threads, such as YLI Pearl Crown Rayon, YLI Candlelight, Superior Threads Halo, and Madeira Décor

Not recommended: woven ribbons, because they are not flexible enough

Ribbon length: 1″–1½″ per knot plus 1″

Note: Contrasting thread is used in photographs to emphasize stitches. Use an invisible thread to hide stitches in finished projects (see Thread, page 10).

French Knot

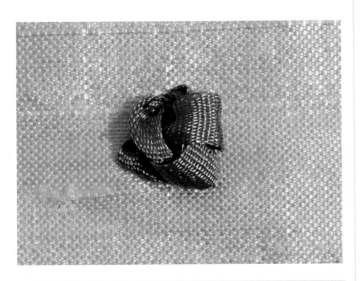

1. Draw small dots on the hooped fabric to indicate knot placement.

2. Choose a 6″ length of 3.5–4mm silk ribbon. Of course, this is more ribbon than necessary to create the stitch, but it allows an ample amount of ribbon to hold on to until you are comfortable with the technique.

3. Secure the thread and tack the ribbon tip to the fabric, with the tail extended to 9 o'clock.

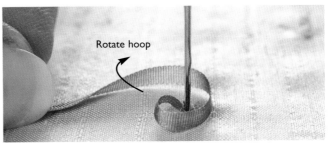

4. Hold the ribbon loosely with the thumb and index finger of your left hand about 2″ from the needle, keeping the ribbon parallel to the fabric. (Holding it at an angle will result in unwanted tension on the ribbon.) Slowly spin the hoop clockwise 4 to 5 times. *Do not be concerned if the ribbon twists at some point, as this only creates interest within the stitch.*

5. As you rotate the hoop, the ribbon winds itself up the needle. Loosen your hold on the ribbon if it begins to hug the needle closely. If the ribbon is wound too tightly, the thread will break in the next step. At this point, the ribbon looks like a small tornado—wider at the top and narrower at the base. Keep a good hold on the ribbon tail.

6. Turn the handwheel, raising the needle out of the stitch, then lower it to the right of the tornado at the 4-o'clock position. The needle penetration should be very close to the ribbon.

7. The ribbon will hug the fabric in the shape of a ball; secure with a few tacking stitches. Add a couple of tiny tacking stitches into the edge of the knot for extra security. Clip the ribbon close to the stitching. Any excess ribbon can be tucked to the back of the fabric with the snag repair tool.

French Knot Bunches

Bunched or grouped French knots can be used to create grape clusters, wisteria, lilacs, and geranium florets. These are just a few suggestions. As you begin to group the knots, new designs will come to mind. Try using a 7mm ribbon, as a comparison with the 3.5–4mm French knots.

1. Draw the French knot bunch diagram on your hooped fabric. The knots are spaced 1/4″ apart.

2. Choose a 6″ length of 3.5–4mm silk ribbon.

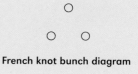

French knot bunch diagram

3. Create a French knot by following Steps 3–6 of the French Knot exercise (page 55). Do not clip the ribbon tail.

4. Twist the ribbon close to the knot and press it against the fabric; this narrows the width of the ribbon. Couch it in place to secure it to the fabric. End the stitching a knot size (approximately ¼˝) away from the first knot.

6. Create the third knot, ending it with the needle positioned in the center of the 3 clustered knots.

5. Create a second French knot and then position the third knot by, again, couching the ribbon in place.

7. Pull the ribbon tail tightly across the front of the needle.

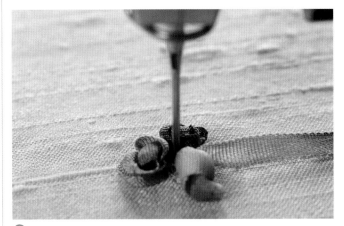

8. Tack the ribbon in place; this will automatically pull the ribbon tail into the center of the cluster to hide it. Clip the excess ribbon and add a few more stitches to lock down any frayed ends.

ruching

R *uching.* Now, there is a term that interests me. The word refers to gathering a ribbon. Historically the technique has been created by hand by inserting stitches zigzag style down the center of a ribbon strip, then pulling them into a gather. The processed ribbon was then used to adorn the edges of fabric or rolled into a floral design to accent a hat or garment. The ruching shown here is actually similar to pleating, with the gathers resulting from pushing pleats into the path of the needle.

Commonly used silk ribbon: 7mm, 13mm, or 32mm

Variations: any woven ribbon at least ½″ wide

Ribbon length: 8″ per 1″ flower

Note: A 1″ ruched spiral will require 6″–8″ of 7mm ribbon. The specific length required depends on the flower being created. Your tension on the ribbon determines whether more or less is needed. If you run short, just tack on additional lengths (see Steps 8–9, page 60).

Note: Contrasting thread is used in photographs to emphasize stitches. Use an invisible thread to hide stitches in finished projects (see Thread, page 10).

Ruched Flowers

For the purpose of this lesson, we will make a carnation. Other flowers that can be created with this stitch are morning glories, hollyhocks, anemones, wild roses ... and the list goes on. Wild roses and poppies will have less of a gather.

1. Draw a ⅞″ circle or the ruching spiral diagram on your hooped fabric.

2. Choose an 8″ length of 7mm silk ribbon.

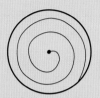

Ruching spiral diagram
(Note: Inner spiral lines are optional.)

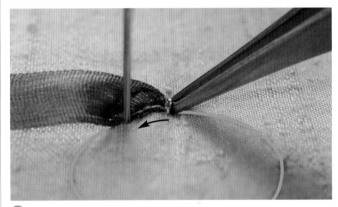

3. Secure the thread and anchor the ribbon to the fabric on the outer edge of the circle. The tail should extend to 9 o'clock. Tack down the lower edge of the ribbon with a couple of stitches to the left.

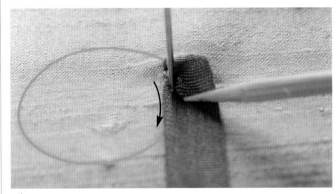

4. Give the hoop a quarter turn clockwise and flip the loose ribbon tail down to 6 o'clock. The ribbon will now be directed toward you, covering the beginning stitches. Tack the left edge of the ribbon in place as you hold it down with a wooden skewer.

5. With the wooden skewer, push tiny pleats into the needle path as you stitch on the ribbon edge.

6. Continue making ribbon pleats around the outer edge of the circle.

7. As the pleated ruching meets the beginning of the circle, route the stitching to the inside of the design as you spiral to the center. The ruffled ribbon should cover the stitching on the outer edge of the circle.

8. If you run out of ribbon before you finish the flower, turn the raw edge of the ribbon under and anchor it to the fabric.

9. Add another length of ribbon in the same manner as Step 3 and 4 and continue the spiral to the end. Color changes within the flower can also be accomplished like this. Continue pleating the ribbon in a spiral toward the center.

10. To finish the flower, give the hoop a full spin and end in a French knot (page 55) at the center of the spiral. Clip the ribbon tail and fluff the center to cover the clipping.

appendix

Free-Motion Exercises

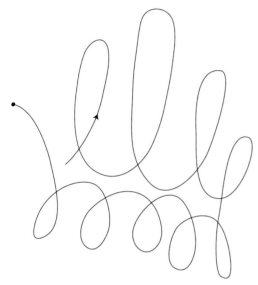

Free-Motion Exercise 1

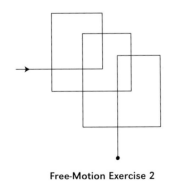

Free-Motion Exercise 2

Free-Motion Exercise 3

Patterns for Play and Practice

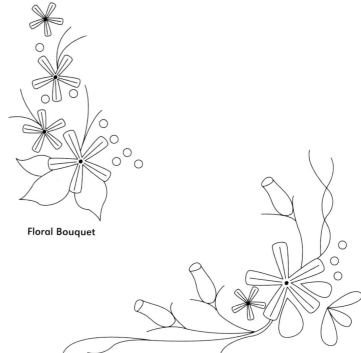

Floral Bouquet

Floral Spray

Floral Corner

Photo Album, by Susan Schrempf, 2006. Corner clusters of rosebuds, daisies, and French knots surround the central floral spray of this album cover. The densely designed bouquet still allows each contributing flower to show its full value. A tightly curled stem stitch spells out the title. The velvet fabric covers an inexpensive damaged cardboard album. Use the patterns provided to practice and play with the motifs in this album.

gallery

Heirloom Pillow, 12″ × 12″,
by Susan Schrempf, 2000.
The variety of basic silk ribbon floral and fern stitches on this cotton pillow combine to create a delicate bouquet. A meandering 4mm silk ribbon secured to the pillow with individual French knots frames the pillow, while feather stitches from the sewing machine add dimension.

Rags to Riches,
by Susan Schrempf, 2001.
Blank garments provide a perfect pallet for embellishing. This discount-store blouse blossomed, literally, when ribbon floss was chain stitched over lace to make a trellis. The elegant background supports lavish 13mm looped flowers, 7mm rosebuds, and grape bunches of 7mm French knots.

Too Cool to Crow, 8″ × 8″,
by Susan Schrempf, 2006. This faux punch-needle
rooster flaunts a fringed tail that was designed with
long loops, using Multi's embellishment yarn from YLI.
Simply cut the loops to create the fringe. Assorted silk
ribbon flowers are gathered in a garland, while royal
purple iridescent satin, edged with rickrack, finishes
the project.

Victorian Holiday, 14″ × 21″,
by Susan Schrempf, 2004.
This quilted batiste holiday
wallhanging is bordered with
emerald green silk dupioni.
The illusionary Christmas tree
is an embroidered motif from
Jim Suzio's Royal Wedding
Collection. Tiny embroidered
cherubs from Cactus Punch
hover near the Spark Organdy
poinsettia tree topper, which was created with the large leaf stitch. Petite
loops of Candlelight thread combine with 2mm lazy daisy stitches and
red glass beads for a rich-looking garland.

Martha's Camisole,
by Susan Schrempf, 2002. This camisole was created from Martha Pullen's book *Lovely Lingerie* and embellished with mirror-imaged embroidery designs from Cactus Punch Signature Series 10—Laura Jenkins Thompson, Heirlooms. Lovely little fantasy ribbon flowers were added to highlight the embroidery. Accents of pearl beads were also added.

Oh! Baby,
by Susan Schrempf, 1999. This adorable, old-fashioned, smocked baby bonnet was machine embellished with a row of vining leaves and individual daisies. The whole design is brought to life by the 4mm silk ribbon lazy daisy stitches.

Nighty Night,
by Susan Schrempf, 1999. Sweet dreams are promised when this soft batiste shortie is worn for slumber. The top front is sewing-machine smocked in pastel thread and edged with English lace. Tiny roses of 7mm peach ribbon were added, using only the center directions of the open rose (see page 44).

Princess Tuffet, 16″ × 16″,
by Susan Schrempf, 2000. This luxurious biscuit pillow,
with a generous 6″ double ruffle, features alternating
machine-embroidered lavender squares and miniature-
violet-motif fabric squares. The floral fabric has been
further defined by three-dimensional violets of silk
ribbon loops and lazy daisy leaves.

Breath of Spring,
by Susan Schrempf, 2003. Roses, pansies, rosebuds, and delphiniums are backed by flowing
ferns and budded branches in this silk ribbon
spring bouquet. Lazy daisy stitches of black
embroidery floss emphasize the depth of the
pansies. Pink scallops created by machine edge
this classic doily.

Crazyquilt Memories,
by Susan Schrempf, 2004. The old lace and
family charm on this Victorian pillow remind us
of the past. Curled ribbon stem stitches provide
the background for petite 4mm silk ribbon
French knots and roses.

Child's Winter Muff,
by Susan Schrempf, 2006. Warm hands
are the reward when they are tucked into
this cozy polar fleece covering. The ribbing
is created at the machine with Superior
Threads Glitter. The stylized poinsettias
were created from 13mm and 7mm
hand-dyed YLI silk ribbon. The leaves and
stems were designed with traveling lazy
daisy stitches, using Superior Threads
Razzle Dazzle combined with YLI Pearl
Crown Rayon.

Heirloom in Copper,
by Susan Schrempf, 2006. The heirloom
technique block shown on point in the
center of this pillow is framed by trian-
gular grids. The grids were created by
chain stitching YLI Copper Candlelight
thread. Bias-cut silk ribbon leaves back
the beautiful 13mm flowers and buds.

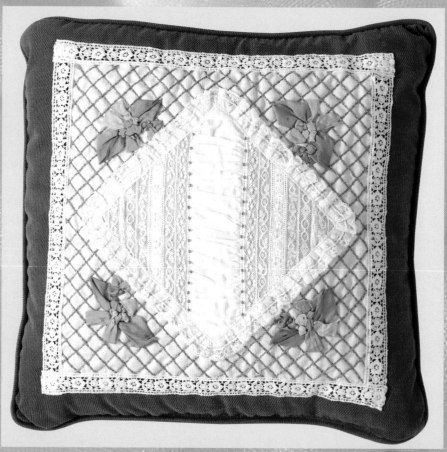

Miss Michelle's Rose Garden,
by Susan Schrempf, 2006. Amid spring green
diamonds nestle Michelle's favorite pink roses. Her garden grows
machine-embroidered, cross-stitched buds and twin 7mm ribbon
rosebuds. Chain-stitched white Razzle Dazzle thread gives the
illusion of raindrops bordering the baby flowers. The quilt pattern
is from "PS I Love You Baby Collection" published by Possibilities:
Milligan and Smith.

Victorian Boot With Flowers,
by Susan Schrempf, 2000.
This elegant, old-world boot
embroidered from the Bernina
Artista 180E is overflowing with
an abundance of silk ribbon flora.
Slender wisps of chain-stitched
1000-denier silk thread enhance
this bouquet's halo.

Summer Picnic,
by Susan Schrempf, 2002. Pussy willows made from 7mm loops are tucked into free-motion-stitched branches of YLI Monet thread. Sunflowers of 4mm golden silk ribbon boast bold French knot centers, while 7mm hollyhocks rise from the center of the embroidered Cactus Punch basket (Basket collection). Free-motion grasses and white Queen Ann flowers add artistic interest.

New York, New York,
by Susan Schrempf, 2006. Pictures of the official greeter of New York City, the Statue of Liberty, are seen through the vinyl pockets of this hot pink tote. Large 13mm Mexican-style flowers celebrate the patina lady.

Mme. Cissy's Shirtdress,
by Susan Schrempf, 2003. Constructed from an antique Simplicity pattern (#2293 from the 1950s), Embroideryarts Roman Leaf Monogram Collection was used to embroider the cross-stitch designs that embellish the skirt, bodice, and sleeves. 4mm ribbon creates the French knot clusters, leaves, and daisies that show off the embroidery.

Miss Bo Peep,
by Susan Schrempf, 2002. This 14″ Madame Alexander doll is clothed in an heirloom dress and pantaloons constructed from a pattern in Martha Pullen's Madame Alexander 14″ Girl Victorian Doll Patterns. The front of the dress features tiny 2mm roses and leaves.

Bold and Beautiful,
by Susan Schrempf, 2006. The heirloom
windowpane quilt block comes alive with
the bold colors of the silk ribbon flowers.
The bright petals invite your eye to look
into the center of the doily for the magic.

Ribbon Stitch Sampler,
by Susan Schrempf, 2004. Floral stitch techniques
are show in each quadrant of this pillow. The
quadrants are divided by the same stitches used
as crazyquilt stitches to show their diversity.

The Garden Jumper,
by Cheryl Weiderspahn, Homestead Specialties, Cochranton, PA, 2002. This is one of many versions of Cheryl's Jumper by the Dozen pattern. Her floral embellishments highlight hems to straps. Open roses, rosebuds, daisies, tulips, and French knots are just some of the flowers found here.

Pioneer Gal's Pincushion,
by Cheryl Weiderspahn, Homestead Specialties, Cochranton, PA, 2004. This novel pincushion began life as a little bird nest. When viewed from the top, the swirled branches seem to dance around the satin cushion as sweet 4mm ribbon flowers pop up to look around.

Mom's Sunflowers,
by Jean Marble, Denver, CO, 2005. Wide, golden, woven-edged ribbon is folded into pointed petals as it travels the surface of these gardenlike blossoms. Silk ribbon has been added to the mix, contributing to the natural appearance.

Victorian Shoe With Flowers,
by Jean Marble, Denver, CO, 2004. Jean's interpretation
of the embroidered boot from the Bernina Artista 180E
shows it filled with a colorful variety of fanciful flowers,
all created with 4mm and 7mm silk ribbon. Stirring
colors, textures, and techniques result in a beautiful
finished work.

Loralie's Daisy,
by Sandra Clark, Aurora, CO, 2002.
Sometimes just a touch of embellishment is all that is needed to make a
statement. Here, a transferred design,
originally created by Loralie Harris of
Loralie Designs, exhibits a crayon-on-
fabric technique. (Daisy, Style #111
from *Loralie Designer Embroidery*,
copyright © 1998-2000 by Loralie
Designs. Courtesy of Loralie Designs.)
The seductive sun hat, in keeping with the mood, displays a lazy
sunflower with leaves, all stitched with 7mm ribbon.

resources

For a list of other fine books from C&T Publishing, ask for a free catalog:

C&T Publishing, Inc.

P.O. Box 1456

Lafayette, CA 94549

(800) 284-1114

Email: ctinfo@ctpub.com

Website: www.ctpub.com

PHOTOGRAPHY SERVICES

C&T Publishing's professional photography services are now available to the public. Visit us at www.ctmediaservices.com.

For quilting supplies:

Cotton Patch

1025 Brown Avenue

Lafayette, CA 94549

(800) 835-4418 or

(925) 283-7883

Email: CottonPa@aol.com

Website: www.quiltusa.com

Note: Fabrics used in the quilts shown may not be currently available as fabric manufacturers keep most fabrics in print for only a short time.

Embroideryarts

Roman Leaf Monogram Collection

17 Fourth Avenue

Nyack, NY 10960

Phone: 888-238-1372

Website: www.embroideryarts.com

Homestead Specialties

Cheryl Weiderspahn, Designer

1883 State Road

Cochranton, PA USA 16314

Phone: 814-425-1183

Website: www.homesteadspecialties.com

HusqvarnaViking

Cactus Punch embroidery collections

Basket Collection

Signature Series 10 – Laura Jenkins Thompson's Heirlooms

VSM Sewing Inc.

31000 Viking Parkway

Westlake, OH 44145

Phone: 800-358-0001

Email: info@husqvarnaviking.com

Website: www.husqvarnaviking.com/us

Jim Suzio Sewing

Royal Wedding embroidery collection

http://betsyelle-ivil.tripod.com

Loralie Designs

1820 S. Morgan Street

Granbury, TX 76048

Phone: 817-573-9382

Website: www.loraliedesigns.com

Madeira USA

30 Bayside Court

Laconia, NH 03246

Phone: 800-225-3001

Website: www.madeirausa.com

Martha Pullen Company

Lovely Lingerie

Madame Alexander 14" Girl

Victorian Doll Patterns

149 Old Big Cove Road

Brownsboro, AL 35741

Phone: 800-547-4176

Website: www.marthapullen.com

Possibilities

Baby Tears pattern from

PS I Love You Baby Collection

8970 E. Hampden Avenue

Denver, CO 80231

Phone: 303-740-6206

Website: www.possibilitiesquilt.com

Prym Consumer USA, Inc.

P.O. Box 5028

Spartanburg, SC 29304

Website: www.dritz.com

Sulky of America

980 Cobb Place Blvd., Suite 130

Kennesaw, GA 30144

Phone: 800-874-4115

Website: www.sulky.com

Superior Threads

87 East 2580 South

St. George, UT 84771

Phone: 800-499-1777

Website: www.superiorthreads.com

YLI Corporation

1439 Dave Lyle Boulevard #16C

Rock Hill, SC 29730

Phone: 803-985-3100

Fax: 803-985-3106

Website: www.ylicorp.com

about the author

Photo by Terry Parker

Susan Schrempf's earliest recollection of her life is of lying on her tummy with crayon in hand, coloring drawings of Christmas flowers while waiting for Santa Claus to arrive. Flowers and creativity have occupied a huge portion of Susan's history, beginning with the drawing of garden flowers from her childhood home.

In her adult life, she has enjoyed a variety of careers—all related to her passion for flora. When she was a young mother of two children, a boy and a girl, her creative tools morphed from drawing pencils to

cones of frosting. Decorated birthday and wedding cakes provided sufficient income for her to remain home and raise her children. Later she opened a chocolate shop, where she further expanded her media for floral creations.

Upon closing the confectionary, a new outlet for floral creativity presented itself. Temporary assistance was needed at a local flower shop. Susan dove in headfirst. Enveloped in the sweet scents, she learned to create corsages, boutonnieres, and beautiful bouquets. Within a month, she became shop manager. In the

years that followed, she educated other florists in design techniques.

When Susan was gifted with a new Bernina sewing machine in 1996, a renewed love for sewing developed that she had not experienced in 25 years. She devoured classes, learning all possible sewing techniques. Heirloom design became her favorite, as it was typically embellished with delicate pastel flowers. She was smitten. With a discerning eye, a love of both sewing and flowers, and incredible attention to detail, Susan set out to create realistic-looking flowers out of silk ribbon that could be made by machine. Her propensity for teaching led her to break down her silk ribbon techniques into steps that could easily be duplicated by others. She has spent the past ten years teaching across the nation, sharing her love of ribbon flowers.

Susan was raised in Arlington Heights, Illinois. There she married and began her family. Twenty-six years ago, after vacationing in Colorado, Susan and her family relocated to Colorado Springs, where she opened her chocolate shop, Sweet Fantasy. While there, she also managed the Air Force Academy flower shops. Susan and her husband currently reside in Aurora, Colorado.

Great Titles

from

C&T PUBLISHING

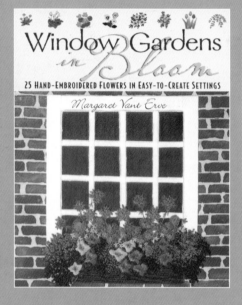

Window Gardens in Bloom
25 HAND-EMBROIDERED FLOWERS IN EASY-TO-CREATE SETTINGS
Margaret Vant Erve

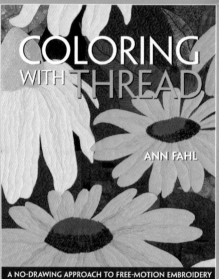

COLORING WITH THREAD
ANN FAHL
A NO-DRAWING APPROACH TO FREE-MOTION EMBROIDERY

The Quilter's Directory of EMBELLISHMENTS
40 step-by-step decorative techniques, from appliqué and embroidery to tassels and trims

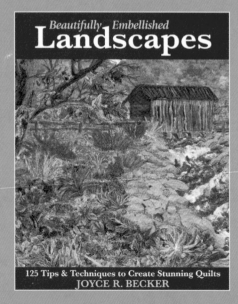

Beautifully Embellished Landscapes
125 Tips & Techniques to Create Stunning Quilts
JOYCE R. BECKER

Creative Beginnings in Machine Embroidery
INNOVATIVE IDEAS FOR EXPERT RESULTS
Patty Albin

fast fun & easy FABRIC POSTCARDS
Franki Kohler
Keepsakes You Can Make & Mail